LAKE OSWEGO JR. HIGH SCHOOL
2500 SW COUNTRY CLUB RD
LAKE OSWEGO, OR 97034
503-534-2335

LYNDON B. JOHNSON

The Presidents of the United States

George Washington
1789–1797

John Adams
1797–1801

Thomas Jefferson
1801–1809

James Madison
1809–1817

James Monroe
1817–1825

John Quincy Adams
1825–1829

Andrew Jackson
1829–1837

Martin Van Buren
1837–1841

William Henry Harrison
1841

John Tyler
1841–1845

James Polk
1845–1849

Zachary Taylor
1849–1850

Millard Fillmore
1850–1853

Franklin Pierce
1853–1857

James Buchanan
1857–1861

Abraham Lincoln
1861–1865

Andrew Johnson
1865–1869

Ulysses S. Grant
1869–1877

Rutherford B. Hayes
1877–1881

James Garfield
1881

Chester Arthur
1881–1885

Grover Cleveland
1885–1889

Benjamin Harrison
1889–1893

Grover Cleveland
1893–1897

William McKinley
1897–1901

Theodore Roosevelt
1901–1909

William H. Taft
1909–1913

Woodrow Wilson
1913–1921

Warren Harding
1921–1923

Calvin Coolidge
1923–1929

Herbert Hoover
1929–1933

Franklin D. Roosevelt
1933–1945

Harry Truman
1945–1953

Dwight Eisenhower
1953–1961

John F. Kennedy
1961–1963

Lyndon Johnson
1963–1969

Richard Nixon
1969–1974

Gerald Ford
1974–1977

Jimmy Carter
1977–1981

Ronald Reagan
1981–1989

George H. W. Bush
1989–1993

William J. Clinton
1993–2001

George W. Bush
2001–2009

LYNDON B. JOHNSON
SUSAN DUDLEY GOLD

Marshall Cavendish
Benchmark
New York

Dedicated to Carol S. Rancourt, who has devoted much of her life to public service as
a member of the Scarborough School Committee and the Scarborough Town Council,
and as a volunteer in many organizations.

With thanks to researcher Lee Burnett for assisting with this book.

Marshall Cavendish Benchmark
99 White Plains Road
Tarrytown, NY 10591-5502
www.marshallcavendish.us

All Internet addresses were correct at the time of printing.

Library of Congress Cataloging-in-Publication Data

Gold, Susan Dudley.
Lyndon B. Johnson / by Susan Dudley Gold.
p. cm. — (Presidents and their times)
Includes bibliographical references and index.
Audience: Grades 7–8
ISBN 978-0-7614-2837-4
1. Johnson, Lyndon B. (Lyndon Baines), 1908–1973—Juvenile literature. 2. Presidents—
United States—Biography—Juvenile literature. 3. United States—Politics and
government—1963–1969—Juvenile literature. I. Title.
E847.G58 2009
973.923092—dc22
[B]
2007038518

Editor: Christine Florie
Publisher: Michelle Bisson
Art Director: Anahid Hamparian
Series Designer: Alex Ferrari

Photo research by Connie Gardner

Cover photo by Roger Violett/The Image Works

The photographs in this book are used by permission and through the courtesy of: *Jupiter Images:*
Ewing Galloway/Index Stock Imagery, 3, 97; *Corbis:* Bettmann, 6, 18, 20, 23, 31, 45, 52, 56, 59, 61,
69, 81, 88, 93, 99 (L&R); Austin Statesman, 35; CORBIS: 40, 48, 66; Yoichi Okamoto, 74; Flip Schulke,
75, 79; Kyoichi Sawada, 84; Wally McNamee, 87; *Getty Images:* Hulton Archive, 25, 62; Time and Life,
41, 51, 70, 72, 98 (R); *Granger Collection:* 36, 37; *AP Photo:* 44, 58, 68; *The Image Works:* Topham, 91;
LBJ Library Image Archives: 8, 9, 10 (T&B), 15, 27, 33, 98 (L).

Printed in Malaysia
1 3 5 6 4 2

CONTENTS

"The presidency has made every man who occupied it, no matter how small, bigger than he was; and no matter how small, not big enough for its demands."
—President Lyndon B. Johnson

THE YOUNG JOHNSON

*R*ifle shots, chaos, and blood marked the beginnings of the presidency of Lyndon Baines Johnson. This big, powerful Texan—the nation's thirty-sixth president—was propelled into office by the November 22, 1963, assassination of President John F. Kennedy. Grief and shock prevailed as Johnson pledged to "faithfully execute the office of president of the United States."

From the beginning of his presidency Johnson set his own course. He took up where Kennedy had left off in the civil rights battle. Under Johnson's leadership, Congress took strong action to further the civil rights of African-American citizens. Some observers claim that Johnson alone had the skill to persuade Congress to pass the nation's most important civil rights act. They say it never would have been adopted in its final form had Johnson not been president.

His campaign to help poor and middle-class citizens transformed America. Johnson launched what became known as the **War on Poverty**. This was a series of programs designed to help the poor obtain a good education, healthy foods, and decent housing. His healthcare programs, Medicare and Medicaid, provided health benefits to elderly and low-income people. It was all part of a master plan Johnson developed to create a "**Great Society**," where everyone had an equal chance to excel.

A war of a different sort, however, brought the president down. Controversy over the Vietnam War split the nation and led to rising discontent with the Johnson administration. By 1968 he had lost the confidence of the American people, and in March he announced his intention not to run for reelection.

Just as praise and protests marked his presidency, Lyndon Johnson's legacy is a mix of blame for a lost war and gratitude for a multitude of programs—from Head Start to public television to those providing housing loans and requiring carmakers to install seat belts—that benefit all Americans.

EARLY YEARS

Lyndon B. Johnson was a driven man whose character was forged by poverty, politics, and overriding ambition. The reconstructed five-room cottage in the Hill Country of western Texas (now a historic site maintained by the National Park Service) looks much as it did when Lyndon Baines Johnson was born there, on August 27, 1908. Life was difficult for the Johnson family at the turn of the century. With no indoor plumbing and no electricity, the family lived simply.

Johnson's parents both came from prominent families. His mother, Rebekah Baines, grew up in Blanco,

Johnson's mother, Rebekah Baines, was from a notable family in Blanco, Texas.

a prosperous town in the Hill Country of Texas. Her father, Johnson's maternal grandfather, Joseph Baines, served in the Texas legislature.

Lyndon Johnson's father, Sam Ealy Johnson Jr., came from a family of farmers and ranchers. Sam's father and uncles had settled in the Hill Country of Texas, raised cotton and cattle, and bought enough property to place them among the largest landowners in the region. Both the Baineses and the Johnsons lost their wealth when floods and droughts destroyed many of the farms in the region.

After going through hard times, Sam Johnson began to make

Sam Ealy Johnson Jr. started a career in farming but soon turned to politics, his real passion.

money from selling his cotton crops. His passion, though, was politics. With encouragement from friends and relatives, he ran for a seat in the Texas House of Representatives—the same seat Joseph Baines had once held—and won. During his first term in office a pretty young reporter—Rebekah Baines—interviewed him. Only a few months later the two married, on August 20, 1907.

After his first term Sam Johnson found he could no longer afford to pay his living expenses in Austin and support a farm in the Hill Country. By then his wife was expecting the couple's first child. Sam Johnson left the political life he loved and returned with his wife to the farm.

Lyndon B. Johnson at eighteen months old.

As a child Johnson enjoyed dressing in outfits that generated attention, especially those that included a Stetson hat.

After Lyndon Johnson was born, on August 27, 1908, his mother spent most of her time with him. She rewarded the toddler with hugs after he recited long poems, a skill Lyndon learned by age three. At four he could read and spell.

Two sisters, Rebekah and Josefa, joined the family in the next few years. Even after they were born, Johnson's mother focused on him. Young Lyndon demanded to be noticed not just by his mother but by everyone. He often ran away or hid while his parents and others searched frantically for him. At age four he began running away to the local school nearby. He read aloud in front of the class—but only if the teacher held him in her lap. Lyndon came to school dressed as a cowboy, complete with a Stetson hat, or in a sailor suit, or short pants and knee stockings. The odd outfits drew attention, which he seemed to like.

In 1913 the family moved to Johnson City, where Lyndon's brother, Sam Houston, and another sister, Lucia, were born. Lyndon's father began making real estate deals, buying and selling property. The family, though still poor, began to earn more money than many others in the community.

TEXAS AND THE CHANGING SOUTH

In the years following World War I, which ended in 1918, the South went through major changes. During and after the war, cotton farms expanded to meet a growing demand. Mexican workers streamed into Texas to pick cotton and fill other farm jobs. An oversupply of cotton, however, led to disaster for many farmers in the early 1920s. For the rest of the decade prices rose and fell, threatening the livelihoods of many farmers in the state.

Once dependent on farming, the Texas economy began to expand into other areas. New technologies, electrical power, irrigation, and the development of oil fields brought jobs and prosperity to the state. Newly established factories attracted workers to cities in the South.

In 1920 women won the right to vote. Also during this time the Ku Klux Klan began attracting members in Texas. The secret society targeted African Americans, immigrants, Catholics, Jews, and other minorities with violence and discrimination. Klan members promoted the "white" race, mainly people of English or Scandinavian heritage of the Protestant faith. Prominent citizens, including doctors, ministers, and government officials, as well as members of the working class, belonged to the Klan.

The Klan and others in the South defended segregation, a system that separated people by race and discriminated against African-American citizens. Klan members terrorized communities by burning crosses on lawns and whipping or hanging opponents. With such fear tactics the Klan took over political races in several Texas districts and became a powerful force in others.

Junior Legislator

In 1918 Lyndon Johnson's father returned to his first passion, politics, and won back his seat in the state legislature. Sam Johnson took a strong stand against the anti-German hysteria that spread throughout the nation after World War I. He also opposed the Ku Klux Klan and spoke forcefully for tolerance and freedom.

Lyndon was tall and thin like his father and had the same large nose and ears. He went with his father to the state house whenever he could. He looked like his father's smaller twin, following him everywhere and copying his every move. The young boy talked with his father's drawl and used the same outgoing manner to greet people. He even mimicked the pose his father used when trying to persuade another legislator to vote his way: nose-to-nose, sometimes grabbing the person's lapel to pull him closer.

Lyndon had considerable talent of his own when it came to persuasion. He convinced much older children to follow his lead at school. Often Lyndon made up a tall tale on the spot that got them all out of trouble. His ability to charm adults amazed his friends. "Lyndon could talk my parents into anything, letting us do anything or go anywhere," one of his childhood friends told Johnson's biographer, Doris Kearns Goodwin.

Both father and son thrived at the legislature and on the campaign trail. Lyndon told Goodwin how much he enjoyed those days:

> I loved going with my father to the legislature. I would sit in the gallery for hours watching all the activity on the floor and then would wander around the halls trying to figure out what was going on. The only thing I loved more was going with him on the trail

during his campaigns for re-election. We drove in the Model T Ford from farm to farm, up and down the valley, stopping at every door. My father would do most of the talking. He would bring the neighbors up to date on local gossip, talk about the crops and about the bills he'd introduced in the legislature. . . . I'd never seen him happier. Families all along the way opened up their homes to us. If it was hot outside, we were invited in for big servings of homemade ice cream. If it was cold, we were given hot tea . . . sometimes I wished it could go on forever.

BROKE AND DISILLUSIONED

After Lyndon's grandparents died, his father bought the old Johnson farm, in 1919. Like his father before him, Sam Jr. mortgaged the farm to pay off debts. In 1920, when his crops failed, the family was forced to sell the farm. The Johnsons lost not only money but also the respect they had had as one of the town's more successful families.

The sudden change in status did not sit well with Lyndon. Used to being the center of attention, he did not like having people look down on him. And he resented his father's failure. The teenager rebelled. After high school he refused to go to college. When his father left town on a business trip, Lyndon and some friends took off for California in a Model T. For a while Lyndon worked at a cousin's law office. The job did not work out, and more than a year later he returned home broke and disillusioned.

After that experience Lyndon Johnson, in 1927 at age eighteen, enrolled at Southwest Texas State Teachers College in San Marcos, Texas. The college, the only one in the Hill Country, accepted students like Johnson, whose poor schooling prevented them from going to a top school.

At first he worked at odd jobs to pay tuition. He soon managed to get a job as an assistant to the college president, Cecil E. Evans, who knew Johnson's parents. Applying his usual charm to win Evans's favor, Johnson quickly became the president's receptionist and adviser and drafted letters for him.

Teaching at Cotulla

In the fall of 1928 Johnson took a teaching job at a small school in southern Texas to help pay for college. Located in the town of Cotulla, the school served poor Mexican immigrants. Like the students, the school was poor, without sports equipment, buses, or a lunchroom. Johnson spent part of his first paycheck buying balls and bats for his students. "I saw hunger in their eyes and pain in their bodies," he later said of the children in his class. "[They] had so little and needed so much. I was determined to spark something inside them, to fill their souls with ambition and interest and belief in the future."

Johnson taught at the school for one term. He never forgot the experience or the poverty he saw in Cotulla. He had those students in mind when he pushed for Head Start and other programs in his campaign as president to fight poverty and give poor children an equal chance at a good life. "I had my first lessons in the high price we pay for poverty and prejudice right here," Johnson told students at the school after he returned in 1966, as president. "No longer can we afford second-class education for children who know that they have a right to be first-class citizens."

College Campaign

Back at college in June 1929 Johnson joined the debate team and worked on the college yearbook and the school newspaper. He

Johnson (right) is photographed with other members of the Southwest Texas State Teachers College debate team.

soon discovered that a small group of insiders controlled most of the activities on campus. This group of students, who were mostly athletes, called themselves the Black Stars. Johnson, who was tall but uncoordinated, had never done well in sports. When he tried to join the group, the members turned him down.

Johnson quickly formed his own society to take on the Black Stars in the next campus election. Called the White Stars, the group set out to win support from others not allied with the Black Stars. The White Stars backed as their candidate the handsome, well-liked Willard Deason. He ran under the campaign slogan "Brains Are Just as Important as Brawn," designed by Johnson to stir opposition to the Black Stars' athletes.

The campaign against the Black Stars turned out to be Johnson's first political triumph. He won by doing what he did best—persuading voters to support his cause. "His greatest forte," said Deason, who became one of Johnson's most loyal friends, "[was] to look a man in the eye and do a convincing job of selling him his viewpoint. In one-on-one salesmanship, Lyndon was the best."

Graduation day in August 1930 was another triumph for Lyndon Johnson. During the ceremony President Evans praised his young aide and predicted "great things [for him] in the years ahead."

Early Political Career

*L*yndon Johnson embarked on his political career during a time of great upheaval in the United States. In the 1920s a great array of new products—cars, household appliances, and other innovations—became part of everyday life. People bought these items on **credit** and invested money in the **stock market**. Though farmers faced hard times, the "Roaring Twenties" brought widespread prosperity to others. Wages and profits rose, and factories produced more goods.

But by the end of the decade, wild spending and unsound investments took a toll. Banks made unwise loans. Some businessmen made huge profits, but many Americans accumulated more and more debt. By the end of the decade, people could not pay their creditors, and the out-of-control spending that had propped up the economy ended abruptly.

On October 29, 1929, a day that would become known as Black Tuesday, the U.S. stock market collapsed, marking the beginning of the Great Depression, the worst economic disaster the world had ever known. It soon spread throughout the globe, causing banks to fail and businesses to close their doors. Up to 15 million Americans lost their jobs. The economy did not regain stability until the early 1940s, when World War II triggered a demand for manufactured goods.

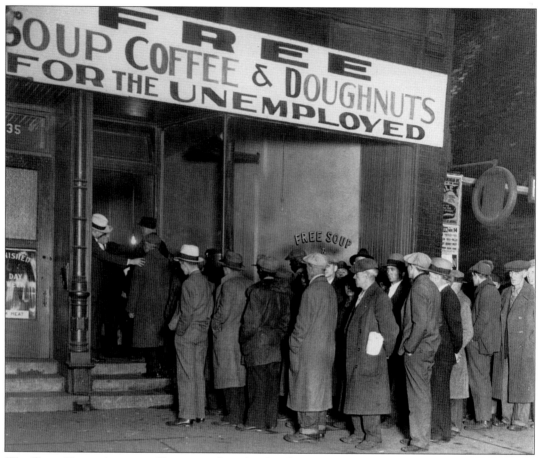

The Great Depression put millions out of work. This Chicago soup kitchen provided three meals a day to the unemployed.

In 1930 Johnson—lucky to have a job—began teaching public speaking and directing the debate team at Sam Houston High School in Houston. A year later U.S. congressman Richard Kleberg offered Johnson a job as his private secretary. The responsibilities of the job were managing the office, arranging tours and meetings with **constituents**, setting the congressman's schedule, researching issues coming up for a vote, and responding to letters and requests. Welly Hopkins, a Texas state senator whose campaign Johnson had managed, recommended the young man for the position. The job took Johnson to Washington, D.C. There he embarked on a journey that would ultimately lead to the White House.

WASHINGTON ROOKIE

In November 1931 Johnson left his job at Sam Houston High School and set out for Washington. He settled into a windowless room below ground level at the Dodge Hotel, within walking distance of the Capitol. He paid twenty dollars a month for the lodgings, which he shared with a roommate. The bathroom was down the hall. The

In 1931 Johnson landed a job at the Capitol (above) as a private secretary to congressman Richard Kleberg.

office Johnson reported to at the Capitol was not much more spacious than his sleeping quarters. At that time congressmen operated out of single-room offices. They had few visitors.

The opportunities open to Johnson more than made up for the cramped office and living space. For a young Democrat from Texas the timing could not have been better. Democrats held the majority in the House for the first time since 1919. Among them was Sam Rayburn, chair of the influential House Committee on Interstate and Foreign Commerce.

Johnson's boss, Richard Kleberg, was a rich playboy who spent most of his time on the golf course when Congress was not in session. "The last thing he [Kleberg] wanted to do was answer letters from constituents crying during the depression," observed Robert Jackson, an aide to another congressman at the time. That left Johnson to answer the mail, research bills, and contact powerful Washington figures to solve constituents' problems. It did not take Johnson long to learn who held the power and where to go to get things done.

He worked seven days a week, arriving at the office earlier than any other aide and staying after hours. Taking to heart the lessons he had learned during the White Stars campaign, Johnson knew that every vote counted. He made it a point to answer every letter from constituents and soon began sending notes congratulating every high school graduate, every newlywed, and every owner of a newly opened business. In the summer of 1932 he hired two aides, Gene Latimer and Luther Jones, to assist him. They were former students who had excelled on the debating team directed by Johnson at Sam Houston High.

LITTLE CONGRESS LEADER

By 1933 Johnson had won his own campaign, as the speaker of Little Congress, a group made up of congressional aides. Modeled on the real Congress, Little Congress debated the same bills that came before the House of Representatives. The only difference was that Little Congress had no constituents and no power to act. Members followed the same parliamentary procedures used in the House. This gave aides practice in public speaking.

Traditionally the speaker position went to the aide who had worked at the Capitol the longest. Johnson overcame that by asking for votes from new aides and workers—letter carriers, security guards, typists, and elevator operators. People in these jobs usually did not vote, but they were allowed to cast ballots if they paid two dollars in dues. The strategy gave Johnson the winning votes but also earned him resentment from senior aides.

Johnson transformed Little Congress into a powerful force. Members of Congress began attending the meetings. Listening to the group's debates on issues helped them prepare for the real debates in Congress. Reporters came to meetings, too. They discovered that the Little Congress debates provided an inside look at where Congress stood on the issues. As speaker of the group Johnson took every opportunity to promote himself and become known to powerful members of Congress. During this time he also became better acquainted with Congressman Sam Rayburn, who had served with his father in the Texas legislature.

WOOING LADY BIRD

In 1934 Johnson traveled to Austin on official business. While there he met Claudia Alta Taylor, the daughter of a wealthy Texas businessman. She had recently graduated from the University of Texas with a degree in arts and journalism. When she was a young child, a nursemaid had commented that Taylor was "purty as a lady bird." Ever since then, people had called her Lady Bird.

Johnson, intrigued by the intelligent, accomplished young woman, set out to win her over in much the same way he did everyone else. On their first date he took her to breakfast and for a drive in the country. "He told me all sorts of things that I thought were extraordinarily direct for a first conversation," Lady Bird recalled later.

For the next several days Johnson spent as much time as he could with the shy and sensitive Lady Bird. The couple met with both sets of parents, and Johnson took her on a tour of the vast ranch owned by his boss, Congressman Kleberg. Back in Washington, Johnson continued to shower attention on Lady Bird. He called, wrote letters, and sent telegrams. Seven weeks after first meeting Lady Bird, Johnson returned to Texas and asked her to marry him. "Sometimes," Lady Bird later said, "Lyndon simply takes your breath away." The couple married in November 1934.

Lady Bird provided Johnson with just the kind

In November 1934 Johnson wed Claudia (Lady Bird) Alta Taylor.

of partner he needed. Always supportive, she had a gracious way about her that made everyone, from powerful political leaders to poor constituents, feel comfortable. Sam Rayburn, who had become Speaker of the House, was a regular guest at the Johnson home. Being Rayburn's protégé opened doors to Johnson that would ordinarily have remained closed to a poor congressional aide from Texas.

Get That Boy a Job

After the stock market crashed in 1929, the nation spiraled into economic despair. With no jobs and no way of supporting their families, people begged on the streets and ate at soup kitchens. In 1932 the Democrats chose Franklin D. Roosevelt, governor of New York, as the party's candidate for president. He pledged to implement "a new deal for the American people" that would ease the financial crisis and help get people back on their feet. Americans, desperate for a change, voted overwhelmingly for Roosevelt.

As soon as he took office, in 1933, Roosevelt introduced the **New Deal**, his plan to cope with the Depression. The New Deal called for a host of federal programs to help the poor and the unemployed. The programs provided emergency relief funds for people in desperate straits, jobs for the unemployed, and help for farmers. A second round of New Deal programs launched the Social Security Administration (which provided guaranteed retirement income for workers) and set up agencies to help people in other ways.

One of the agencies was the National Youth Administration (NYA), which helped young people find jobs and continue their education. In 1935 Lyndon Johnson decided to leave his

Part of President Roosevelt's plan to ease the Great Depression was to get Americans back to work. Here, Roosevelt (on right) greets farmers in Georgia.

congressional post and apply for a job as administrator of the Texas NYA. Roosevelt had already promised the job to someone else, but Texas congressmen Sam Rayburn and Maury Maverick persuaded the president to give the post to Johnson. Not quite twenty-seven, Johnson became the youngest state director of the NYA in the country.

He approached the job with his usual energy. "I work seventeen hours a day," Johnson told his staff. "All I ask you to work is sixteen, and we'll get that boy on the streetcorner a job." Unlike other NYA directors in the South, Johnson quietly included African Americans among the thousands of "boys on the streetcorner" who benefited from the program. Johnson saw to it that his efforts did not go unnoticed. His invitation to Eleanor Roosevelt to visit Texas not only drew attention to his accomplishments but also turned the first lady into a Johnson supporter. Through his NYA work, he met hundreds of powerful people who later helped him in his political career.

CAMPAIGNING FOR CONGRESS

Lyndon Johnson had been on the job at NYA for a year and a half when James P. Buchanan, a Democratic congressman from Texas, suddenly died. Buchanan had represented the Tenth District, which included the Hill Country, Johnson's homeland. Each state is divided into sections, or districts. Voters in each district are entitled to elect one member to the U.S. House of Representatives.

The Tenth District also included Austin, where Johnson lived as director of the NYA. The list of possible successors included Buchanan's widow, his campaign manager, and several state officials, including a state senator and an assistant state attorney general. Johnson's name did not appear in the local paper's list of potential candidates.

Johnson's father advised him to announce his candidacy for the seat before anyone else had a chance to do so. He did exactly that in February 1937. With ten thousand dollars from his father-in-law and the support of the influential attorney and former Texas state senator Alvin Wirtz, Johnson set out on a remarkable forty-two-day campaign to win the election.

According to biographer Doris Kearns Goodwin, "Johnson poured massive energy into those forty-two days of campaigning—a torrential, seemingly tireless flow of personal activity and labor which no other candidate could match." During the campaign Johnson shook the hands of thousands of voters. He made a connection with people. Texan Lera Thomas, whose husband served in Congress with Johnson and who later held

Johnson ran for a seat in Congress in 1937. This campaign poster touts Johnson as someone who "Gets Things Done."

the same seat after her husband's death, described Johnson's approach. "If he was speaking to you, he would completely absorb you," she said. "He would talk directly to one person. . . . So he was very convincing in that way."

Johnson immediately portrayed himself as a "Roosevelt man" by supporting the president. He spoke out in favor of Roosevelt's plan to pack the Supreme Court with justices who supported the New Deal. After the Supreme Court's Republican majority ruled against many New Deal proposals, Roosevelt called for the retirement of all justices over the age of seventy. If they did not retire, Roosevelt proposed that he be allowed to appoint a new justice to serve along with each aging justice. That would have allowed the president to increase the size of the Court to fifteen justices. The justices appointed by Roosevelt would, of course, favor the New Deal.

The plan would eventually be shot down by Congress, but at the time, voters in the Tenth District overwhelmingly supported the popular Roosevelt. Several other candidates also supported the Roosevelt proposal, but none spoke out as enthusiastically about it as Johnson did. The strategy set him apart from the seven other candidates. It also won him the support of prominent Roosevelt supporters.

Johnson's tactics brought him national publicity. An article in the *New York Times* on March 7, 1937, noted that Johnson "stood squarely behind the Roosevelt [court-packing] proposal." It reported that the election put the voters in the Tenth District in the position of being the first in the nation to weigh in on the issue.

With only two days to go before the election, Johnson had an attack of appendicitis. He was in the hospital recovering from surgery when his victory made national news. In a page-one story the *New York Times* announced JOHNSON, BACKING ROOSEVELT'S COURT PLAN, WINS SEAT IN CONGRESS IN TEXAS ELECTION. The article reported that the "youthful" candidate "who shouted his advocacy of President Roosevelt's court reorganization all over the tenth Texas district . . . happily received reports of an emphatic victory over seven opponents." Johnson's home county of Blanco gave him almost three times the votes cast for all the other candidates combined. Only one out of nine citizens in the district voted in the election, however. In the final tally Johnson won 8,280 votes. His nearest competitor, Merton Harris, polled 5,111, more than 3,000 votes behind Johnson.

IN THE HOUSE

$\mathcal{C}$ongressman Lyndon Johnson began his next campaign for re-election to Congress the day after winning his first election. He immediately sent letters to all his opponents, offering his services to them. He then set about firming up his relationship with President Franklin D. Roosevelt. Johnson's election, at least in the press, had been billed as the first public vote for Roosevelt's Supreme Court scheme. Roosevelt, who had doubtless followed the election from Washington, agreed to meet with the young congressman during a stop in Texas shortly after Johnson's election. Johnson stood close to the president in newspaper photographs taken during the Texas visit.

At Roosevelt's urging, Johnson was appointed to the powerful House Committee on Naval Affairs. The president helped Johnson in other ways as well. Most important, he introduced the young Johnson to the powerful leaders of the day. Soon he and Lady Bird became regulars at social gatherings of members of Roosevelt's inner circle, the New Dealers. He entertained them with his stories of larger-than-life Texas characters.

Abe Fortas, a New Dealer whom Johnson, while president, appointed to the U.S. Supreme Court, first met Johnson at these social events. "If Lyndon Johnson was there," Fortas told historian Robert A. Caro, "a party would be livelier. The moment he walked in the door, it would take fire."

THE DEAL MAKER

Johnson made good use of his relationships with these men to win approval for a dam that would bring electric power to his

Johnson (right) meets with President Roosevelt (left) and Texas governor James Allred (center) during Roosevelt's visit to Texas on May 13, 1937.

constituents. It and another multimillion-dollar deal were among the major triumphs of his early career. The dam was part of the Lower Colorado River Authority, a state project to control flooding and provide electric power to a large section of Texas that included Austin and the Hill Country.

Providing power to rural Texas made a huge impact on the lives of his constituents and filled Johnson with pride. "I think of all the things I have ever done," he wrote in 1959, "nothing has ever given me as much satisfaction as bringing power to the Hill Country of Texas."

Turning on the Lights

By 1930 most U.S. cities and large towns had electrical service. Those living on farms and in rural areas did not. There were not enough people living in these areas to pay the costs of installing electricity. Residents in town turned on lights with a flip of the switch and used a variety of electrical appliances to make their lives easier. Meanwhile farmers had to do all their chores by hand: milking cows, hauling water, picking crops, and washing clothes. Dim kerosene lamps offered little light at night.

In 1935, under Roosevelt's New Deal, the Rural Electric Administration began bringing electricity to rural America. As a result, life on the farm became much brighter—in more ways than one. Farmers installed lights, indoor bathrooms, and central heating. Chores became easier with electric-powered farm equipment and household appliances. Farms became more productive as electricity brought irrigation, refrigeration, and bigger, more effective machines.

The Hill Country, where Johnson grew up, was among the last areas in Texas to receive electricity. The day the lights came on marked the dawn of a new era for the region.

Next Johnson brokered an even better deal. As part of the arrangement Johnson's old ally Alvin J. Wirtz was appointed the Under Secretary of the Interior, the second in command at the department in charge of land and natural resources. Johnson himself was given say in several federal contracts. The largest was a $100 million project to build the Corpus Christi Naval Air Station. With his direct link to Roosevelt, Johnson had more influence as a young freshman representative than any other member of the Texas delegation.

Johnson used his influence to funnel more federal money to the Tenth District. Millions of dollars in **federal subsidies** went to Hill Country cotton farmers to prop up falling prices and to build roads to get crops to market faster. In Austin, federal money paid for an addition to City Hall, a new wing on the city's hospital, streetlights, and a new building for the airport. Other Texas communities

As congressman, Johnson won a major coup in obtaining a grant for a new housing project in his home district.

benefited as well. His biggest coup came when the first New Deal public-housing project grant was awarded to the city of Austin. "He got more projects, and more money for his district, than anyone else," Corcoran, Roosevelt's aide, said later. "He was the best Congressman for a district that *ever was*."

Defeat and War

Johnson's grateful constituents returned him to office when he ran for a full two-year term in 1938. In Congress, however, Johnson was uncharacteristically silent. He rarely spoke on a bill and seldom introduced his own bills. He was only one of 435 members, and power in the House depended on seniority. Waiting for years to gain a position of power made him "terribly restless and unhappy," he told writer Doris Kearns Goodwin.

Another death and another chance at a seat—this time in the Senate—set him eagerly on the campaign trail again in April 1941. When Texas senator Morris Sheppard died, Johnson decided to run for his seat. He followed the path he had so successfully traveled during his first congressional campaign. This time, however, Texas voters were not as supportive of Roosevelt as they had been. The president's popularity had declined along with the economy, and the threat of war was overhanging the nation.

Johnson's opponent, the sitting governor of Texas, Wilbert L. O'Daniel, had a large base of supporters in the state. When the final votes were counted, O'Daniel won the election with a 1,311-vote lead. Though crushed by the loss, Johnson still had his seat in the House. He had hung onto the seat during the campaign and returned to Washington as a congressman rather than as the senator he had hoped to be.

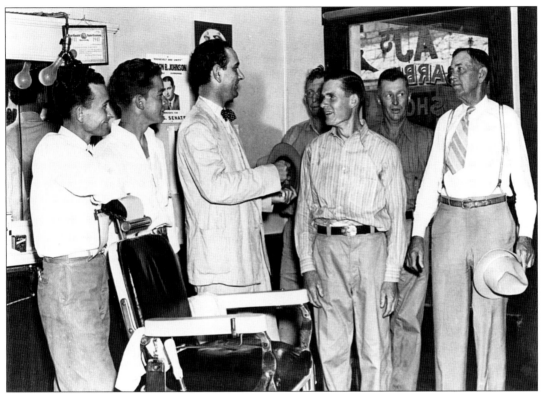

Johnson (center, in suit) campaigns in Texas for a seat in the U.S. Senate.

WAR ON THE HORIZON

While Johnson was on the campaign trail, war consumed Europe and threatened the rest of the world. Germany, under Adolf Hitler and the Nazis, invaded Poland in 1939. War spread to the rest of Europe in 1940, when the Germans seized Denmark, Norway, Belgium, the Netherlands, and France and targeted the United Kingdom. Later that year Japan, Italy, and Germany became allies against the rest of Europe. During 1940 and 1941

As Johnson campaigned for his senate seat, World War II raged in Europe. Here German soldiers invade Poland in September 1939.

the United States strove to remain neutral. Still in the grip of the Depression, the country focused much of its attention on the economy. America did, however, provide arms and ships to Britain.

America entered the war after Japan attacked Pearl Harbor on December 7, 1941. Johnson immediately enlisted in the navy,

ATTACK ON PEARL HARBOR

On December 7, 1941, shortly before 8:00 A.M., Japanese planes dropped bombs on the U.S. fleet at Pearl Harbor, Hawaii. The surprise attack left more than 2,400 Americans dead. The bombs sank or damaged twenty-one ships of the U.S. Pacific fleet. More than 1,100 military personnel and civilians suffered injuries in the bombing. Speaking to a shocked American public and Congress the following day, President Franklin D. Roosevelt said that December 7 would forever be "a date which will live in infamy." Within one-half hour of Roosevelt's broadcast the U.S. Congress declared war against Japan. Three days later America entered the war against Germany and Italy as well.

the first congressman to join the service after the president's call to war. As a candidate for the Senate, Johnson had pledged, "If the day ever comes when my vote must be cast to send your boy to the trenches, that day Lyndon Johnson will leave his Senate seat and go with him."

After training, Johnson headed for Australia and New Zealand as a lieutenant commander. He won a Silver Star for his work as an observer of bomber missions in the South Pacific in 1942. Later that year Roosevelt ordered all members of Congress who were in the service to return to Washington, D.C. On July 16, 1942, Johnson was released from active duty and returned to resume his responsibilities as a U.S. congressman. Johnson had planned to run in 1942 for the Senate seat held by O'Daniel, but the war got in the way. Instead he settled for his familiar seat in the House.

After Johnson came home from the war, he and his wife had two daughters, Lynda in 1944 and Luci in 1947.

SENATE RACE OF 1948

The ailing Franklin Roosevelt died of heart failure on April 12, 1945, and Vice President Harry S. Truman took his place as president. By that point many of the New Dealers had left government, and conservative forces in Congress had dismantled many of the programs Roosevelt had set up. The base of power began to shift toward business interests that wanted to limit Roosevelt's social programs.

Johnson still had his eye on the Senate seat held by O'Daniel who, according to rumor, would not run for reelection in 1948. To Johnson's dismay, Texas governor Coke Stevenson, fondly known as "Mr. Texas," announced that he planned to run for the seat. Stevenson, a cowboy, lawyer, judge, and former speaker of the Texas house of representatives, was the most popular governor in the history of Texas. Some called him "the most potent political force in the state."

Despite the odds Johnson decided to risk his political career on a shot at the Senate seat. This time he would not be able to fall back on his congressional post, since that would be up for election at the same time.

The two candidates spent most of their efforts trying to win the Democratic primary in July. The winner would almost certainly win the state contest for the seat, since Texas had been a Democratic stronghold for decades.

Stevenson was an old-school politician. His campaign strategy had always been to get out and meet voters. During his 1944 reelection campaign for governor, Stevenson did little active campaigning and spent little money. Despite this, Texans had returned him to office with 85 percent of the vote.

Johnson, as the underdog, determined to use every technological advantage he could. He began his campaign with a radio address in which he went on the attack. The most unusual tool—and the one that brought him the most attention—was his use of a helicopter on the campaign trail.

Joe Mashman served as Johnson's pilot. "The helicopter wasn't just a means of getting [Johnson] from place to place," he said in a 1974 interview. "It would draw people." And while people were standing around the helicopter, Johnson shook their hands and gave his campaign speech. "We always tried to land right next to the courthouse or the center of town," Mashman said. While in

These two images capture on his helicopter campaign for the Senate in 1948 in his home state of Texas.

flight, Johnson studied the critical issues facing the area and reviewed a list of people in the community who had written to him Mashman recalled:

> *We covered as many as thirty towns a day and . . . we'd just fly over . . . a number of smaller towns on the way. . . . As we'd fly over the town, we'd slow down and . . . [Johnson would say], "This is your friend, Lyndon Johnson. I'm sorry we can't land today, but I want you to know that I'm up here thinking of you and appreciate your kind letter and comments. I just want you to be sure and tell your friends to vote for me at election time." And then we'd go on.*

LANDSLIDE LYNDON

Johnson continued his attacks on Stevenson. By election eve the two candidates were almost evenly matched. The final tally on

July 24, election day, gave Stevenson the lead, with 40 percent of the vote. Johnson received 34 percent. Other candidates in the primary won the remaining votes. Since no candidate received more than 50 percent of the votes, a runoff election between Johnson and Stevenson was scheduled for August 28.

The election was so close that it took several days for officials to announce the results. On August 31 Stevenson had a 349-vote lead, with supposedly only about 40 votes yet uncounted. But on September 5 the *New York Times* reported that Johnson had pulled ahead by 58 votes.

The conservative *Dallas Morning News* called for an official inquiry into the election. Stevenson questioned the sudden appearance of last-minute gains for his opponent. Others charged that Johnson had stolen the election—tampered with ballots and paid for votes. Johnson, for his part, asked that the Federal Bureau of Investigation look into the matter.

The State Democratic Executive Committee awarded the primary to Johnson on September 13, 1948. Johnson officially won the primary by eighty-seven votes, leading critics to call him "Landslide Lyndon."

Senator Johnson is photographed in his new office in 1948.

On election day Democrats swept the state, and Johnson polled more than twice as many votes as his Republican opponent. Nationally, Democrats won a majority in the Senate. In the end the Senate Rules Committee upheld Johnson's election and certified three other seats that had been contested in the same national election. Despite Stevenson's vows to continue his battle for reelection the matter was eventually dropped.

IN THE SENATE Four

With the election behind him, Johnson got to work building a power base. The Senate, like the House, delegated powerful leadership positions and committee assignments based on seniority. Johnson, as a freshman senator, had to start from the bottom.

Following his usual pattern, he worked long hours and accepted the job of majority whip in 1951. The position had little power, but it brought him to the attention of Democratic leaders. As whip, he was responsible for rounding up members to vote on issues of importance to the party leadership.

During the 1952 elections Johnson worked for Democratic candidates in Texas. His efforts did not go unrewarded. When the Senate shifted to Republican control with a one-vote majority, Johnson made a bid to become minority leader in 1953. With support from Senate leader Richard Russell and others, Johnson easily won the post. He used the position to convince senators to alter the seniority system slightly by allowing every new member a seat on a major committee. That action earned him the gratitude of members of the freshman class who would later become strong leaders.

Hubert H. Humphrey, who later served as President Johnson's vice president, was amazed at Johnson's ability to form relationships with both liberals and conservatives, northerners and southerners, "and still not be one of them." He said Johnson "always had a political finger up to the political temperature and the environment . . . he was, I think, biding his time . . . and building his contacts. Not breaking with the South—but rather

Johnson had the ability to forge relationships with all of the senators, regardless of their home region or party affiliation. Here Johnson confers with Republican senators Wayne Morse (right) and Leverett Saltonstall (left) in January 1951.

bending the southern attitude somewhat to his will, staying close enough to the southern leadership so that they trusted him, and so that he could work with them."

Among the challenges Johnson took on in his new post was how to stop Senator Joseph McCarthy's ruthless campaign to uncover communists. The Wisconsin senator targeted federal workers he suspected of being communists or of sympathizing with them. To many, his hearings resembled witch hunts.

Senator Joseph McCarthy testifies before the Senate subcommittee in an effort to link others to communism.

McCarthy ruined people's lives without producing any evidence of their guilt. Many leaders did not approve of McCarthy's tactics, but they feared they would be seen as "soft" on communism if they opposed him.

According to Abe Fortas, a longtime Johnson ally, Johnson played a key role in stopping McCarthy. As minority leader, Johnson emboldened the wary senators when he proposed that McCarthy be censured for dishonoring the Senate with his tactics.

Joseph McCarthy, the Cold War, and Communism

In the 1940s and 1950s the United States and the Union of Soviet Socialist Republics (U.S.S.R.) became involved in a power struggle. This period of conflict and tension was known as the cold war. The two superpowers did not battle each other directly, but they were involved in a number of conflicts, starting with the Korean War in 1950.

The U.S.S.R. was a communist nation. Its people lived under communism, a system that divided all property among the nation's citizens. The government provided for most of their needs, including health care and higher education. Soviet leaders, however, controlled practically every aspect of life in the countries that formed the U.S.S.R. (including present-day Russia). They banned religion, censored the news, and jailed or killed those who did not agree with them.

U.S. citizens lived under a capitalistic democracy. This system was very different from communism. People owned their property and operated independently from the government. The U.S. Constitution guaranteed freedom of speech and protected those who disagreed with the nation's leaders.

During the Korean War (1950–1953) the Soviets sided with communists in northern Korea, while the United States supported anticommunists in southern Korea. The war ended with a truce that split the country into two nations, North Korea under communist rule and a capitalist South Korea.

Tensions between the superpowers increased when Soviet leaders threatened to take over the United States. Communism became the enemy for many Americans. In February 1950 Senator Joseph McCarthy, a Republican from Wisconsin, began a fierce campaign to uncover communist spies he claimed held U.S. government posts. He never produced any hard evidence, but he bullied and harassed those he accused during hearings before his Senate subcommittee. Afraid of being targets themselves, even the nation's leaders did not take steps to stop McCarthy.

In January 1954 the American people saw the hearings firsthand on television. It was the first time such hearings had been televised to a national audience. Stunned at McCarthy's tactics, viewers began to turn against him. Finally, in December 1954, the Senate voted to censure McCarthy, ending his reign of terror.

After Johnson's suggestion every Democratic senator present voted to censure McCarthy. The measure passed with a vote of 67 to 22, spelling the beginning of the end for the fiery Wisconsin senator. Fortas later said McCarthy's hearings had threatened the nation's freedom.

MAJORITY LEADER

In 1955 Johnson became **majority leader** when an independent cast his vote with the Democrats, giving them a one-vote lead in the Senate. Johnson used the new position to change the way the

THE JOHNSON TREATMENT

Lyndon Johnson mastered his own style of persuasion early in his career. He used it to win support for his causes. A mix of southern charm, haggling, physical intimidation, and arm-twisting, the technique came to be known as the Johnson Treatment. When Johnson spotted a person whose vote he needed, he stood practically nose-to-nose, looked the person in the eye, and outlined his arguments forcefully. There was no escape for the unfortunate target of the treatment. Sometimes Johnson even grabbed the person by the lapels, pulling him in closer to drive his points home.

Authors Rowland Evans and Robert Novak described the Johnson Treatment. They said Johnson "moved in close" to the person he was talking to. He widened and narrowed his eyes, then raised and lowered his eyebrows. Johnson spoke rapidly and mocked, accused, or complained to his target. At times he used humor or careful logic. He often showed the person an assortment of clippings and statistics to make his point. No one was allowed to interrupt his speech. The treatment, according to the writers, was "an almost hypnotic experience" that left the listener "stunned and helpless."

Senate operated, and in the process put himself at the seat of power. Back then, Humphrey noted, the Senate "was a closed shop, . . . you were either in or out." As a liberal who promoted civil rights for African Americans, Humphrey was most definitely in the "out" category. "We [liberals] were looked upon as wild men, as dangerous radicals."

But not by Lyndon Johnson. He understood that he would need members from both sides of the aisle if he were to cement his power. He volunteered to take on the "burden" of assigning office space. Once that was approved, he parceled out prime offices as rewards to his supporters and as a way to influence others. Johnson also gained control over the **Democratic Policy Committee**, which he put in charge of scheduling bills. Senators who wanted special treatment on a bill—whether to rush it along or slow it down—had to come to Johnson with their requests.

Step by small step, Johnson solidified control under his leadership. "It did not occur to his powerful associates—respectfully consulted in every move—that from such insubstantial resources Lyndon Johnson was shaping the instruments that would make him arbiter, and eventually, the master of the United States Senate," historian Doris Kearns Goodwin wrote.

Johnson also managed relations between the Senate and the president. Republican president Dwight D. Eisenhower, a moderate, often had an easier time working with Johnson than with members of his own party, because many of the Republicans opposed the civil rights measures Eisenhower had proposed.

Early Coup

One of Johnson's earliest coups as majority leader came when he convinced the Senate to increase spending for public housing. In 1955 President Eisenhower's administration proposed a housing bill that would have provided only 70,000 units over two years. Everyone, including the Democrats, expected the president's bill to pass. Instead, the Senate approved a Democratic bill Johnson supported that authorized federal funds for a minimum of 200,000 units over four years.

The episode demonstrated the skill, attention to detail, and single-mindedness that made Johnson a master politician. The morning before Congress was to vote on the issue, the press had predicted that Johnson could be facing a big defeat. Johnson was an expert at counting votes. He knew that the vote would be extremely close and that he would have to make sure every supporter of the Democratic bill was on the floor. Senator Hubert Humphrey, a certain vote for the Democrats, was on his way back from Minnesota and had not yet arrived when the Senate prepared to take the vote. Johnson stalled the action while he called the control tower at National Airport to clear the way for the plane that carried Senator Humphrey. When the dust cleared, the Senate had voted down Eisenhower's plan 44 to 38 and had approved the Democratic version 60 to 25. Humphrey had hopped in the car Johnson had waiting for him at the airport, sped to Capitol Hill, and run up the Senate steps just in time to cast his vote.

Humphrey later commented, "I only can imagine what it was like with Johnson . . . on that telephone, really almost commanding the controllers at the tower to get the plane in. He had called our office to find out what the flight num-

A skilled politician, Johnson was able to use his power and influence to get the job done.

ber was and what time I had left Minneapolis, what plane I was on. And he did get the plane in."

The *New York Times* called the vote "a triumph for the democratic floor leader, Senator Lyndon B. Johnson of Texas."

The stress of Johnson's high-pressure job eventually caught up with him. On July 2, 1955, the majority leader suffered a massive heart attack. After spending a month in Bethesda Naval Hospital, he went home to his ranch in Texas to recuperate. Johnson did not return to the Senate until December.

Civil Rights (1957)

Civil rights proved to be the greatest challenge to Johnson's majority leadership. During the 1940s and early 1950s white southerners who controlled Congress engineered the defeat of six civil rights bills. Many southerners argued that individual states should have the right to manage their own affairs. They often used the states' rights argument to preserve segregation, a system of laws that required African Americans to be separate from whites.

In 1956 African-American students in Florida boycott busing to protest segregation.

In the mid-1950s African Americans began to push harder for equal rights. At that time the South had laws that banned African-American children from going to school with white students. Other laws kept African Americans out of hotels, swimming pools, and other gathering spots where whites went. These laws, called Jim Crow laws, enforced segregation, the separation of people by race. The laws also kept African Americans from voting and denied them many opportunities open to white citizens.

The U.S. Supreme Court struck down segregation in public schools in the 1954 *Brown* v. *Board of Education of Topeka, Kansas* case. Encouraged, civil rights activists led by the Reverend Martin Luther King Jr. participated in a successful bus boycott in Montgomery, Alabama. They protested segregation in demonstrations and marches throughout the South. Pressure for change began to mount from a public outraged at the violent actions of southern whites against the Court-ordered school desegregation.

In 1957 the Republican president Dwight D. Eisenhower proposed a civil rights act. The act called for the creation of a civil rights division of the Justice Department and a federal Civil Rights Commission. In addition, federal prosecutors would have the power to enforce African Americans' right to vote, and the attorney general would be able to take action against schools that refused to desegregate.

Johnson supported civil rights, but he knew that pushing for a strong bill would anger many Democrats in the South. He worked out a deal with southerners to pass a weakened bill and convinced liberal western members to pass it in exchange for support for a dam they wanted built. The final bill set up the two federal offices but placed juries in charge of deciding the fate of violators. Southern jurors, almost all of whom were white, rarely ruled in favor of black Americans.

Despite its weaknesses the bill did break ground as the first civil rights legislation to be enacted by Congress in eighty-two years. Johnson received credit for keeping the Democratic Party together and for pushing the through landmark civil rights legislation.

THE VICE PRESIDENCY

$\mathcal{L}$yndon Johnson's Senate successes made him a familiar figure on the television evening news. The presidency seemed the next logical step for a man with his overriding ambition.

On January 3, 1960, in its Sunday edition, the *New York Times* reported that senators Hubert H. Humphrey and John F. Kennedy were the first two Democrats to announce their candidacy for president. The paper mentioned three other Democrats as possible contenders: Adlai Stevenson, who had run and lost to Dwight D. Eisenhower in the 1952 and 1956 elections; Senator Stuart Symington of Missouri; and Lyndon Johnson.

The article described Johnson, then fifty-one, as "the architect of the policy of 'responsible cooperation' with the Republican President by the Democratic-controlled Congress." In the *Times* story Johnson seemed to be positioning himself as a moderate. The *Times* went on to note that Americans had not elected a southern president since the 1800s.

The Democratic candidate would face Republican Richard Nixon, the sitting vice president under Eisenhower.

Johnson stayed out of the primaries and dedicated himself to his work in the Senate. Those on the campaign trail faced daily scrutiny and criticism, while he remained untouched. Johnson hoped that at the convention he could step in as a compromise candidate. Meanwhile, Kennedy used the time to pile up wins at Democratic **primaries**, putting him in the lead.

Presidential hopeful John F. Kennedy learns of his victory over Senator Hubert Humphrey in the West Virginia primary on June 11, 1960.

Johnson waited until the **Democratic Convention** in July to make his move. On July 5 he issued his formal announcement that he intended to challenge Kennedy, the front-runner, as the party's pick for president. Johnson touted himself as a southerner who could attract northern as well as southern votes. "His great strength and his great weakness are that he is a political operator of enormous [skill]," the *New York Times* noted; "a master of the art of compromise and one of the most effective parliamentary leaders of modern times." Even with Johnson's strengths, the newspaper placed Kennedy "far ahead in delegate strength" and noted that he was "so close to the winning line that it is difficult now to see how he can lose."

At the Convention

The Democrats held their convention in Los Angeles that year. Convention delegates usually voted several times before finally agreeing on one candidate. On July 13 the voting began, with 409 votes cast for Johnson. The long process continued as delegates rose to promote other candidates, demonstrated for their favorites, and cast their ballots.

As the Kennedy nomination neared, Johnson sat in his hotel room "confidently waiting for the second and third ballot." He watched in shock as Kennedy's supporters rallied to give their candidate the nomination on the first ballot. The young senator from Massachusetts captured 806 votes as other candidates released their supporters to vote for him.

Kennedy knew that as a young northern liberal, he would need all the help he could get to win votes in the South. Johnson, a well-established Texan politician, could garner southern votes. Despite opposition from many of his supporters, Kennedy asked Johnson to run as vice president. The convention shouted a hearty vote of support for Johnson, the only nominee for the post. In his acceptance speech Johnson said he "could not say no" to his party's "call to serve" the nation. He extolled Kennedy's "character, quality, and greatness." Then he graciously asked the convention to take a voice vote to give Kennedy unanimous support as the party's presidential candidate.

Johnson's acceptance of Kennedy's offer to run on the Democratic ticket as vice president surprised many of his friends and associates. They were well aware of his overreaching ambition to be number one. His friend Abe Fortas later admitted that Johnson's decision "startled" him. Even Kennedy said he was surprised

Senator Johnson accepts the vice-presidential nomination from the Democratic Party at the 1960 national convention.

by Johnson's acceptance of the offer, according to a front-page *New York Times* story.

Johnson explained his decision by saying, "Power is where power goes." During the convention Kennedy pledged to expand the duties of the vice presidency and to allow Johnson to be part of the national leadership.

The two men campaigned hard that fall. Johnson spent a great deal of time winning over southern voters, who had expressed doubts about electing a young northerner who was also a Roman Catholic. As a southerner and an expert politician

Johnson succeeded in delivering the vote in Texas and wide margins in Louisiana and Georgia. Without support from those states, the Democrats would have lost the election.

When the voters went to the polls in November, they chose Kennedy and Johnson as their new leaders. The vote was among the closest in American history, with 49.7 percent for the Democratic ticket and 49.6 percent for the Republican Nixon.

After a close race, Kennedy and Johnson were voted into the White House.

OUT TO PASTURE

Johnson may have been expecting to transform his role in the White House as he had done in the Senate. If so, he had an unpleasant surprise awaiting him. Kennedy, like all the presidents before him, kept the power of his office tightly under his own control. Johnson was relegated to minor posts and menial assignments. As chair of the Space Council, however, he pushed hard for Kennedy's mission to put a man on the moon.

Johnson soon discovered that he no longer had the power he had enjoyed as Senate majority leader. He hoped to preside over meetings of the Democratic caucus in the Senate, but members rejected the proposal. The refusal crushed him. He later confided to historian Doris Kearns Goodwin, "The Vice-Presidency is filled with trips around the world, chauffeurs, men saluting, . . . but in the end, it is nothing. I detested every minute of it."

"A Loss That Cannot Be Weighed"

One thousand days into his term of office, President John F. Kennedy went to Texas on a precampaign trip. He aimed to win southern support for his reelection bid. First Lady Jacqueline Kennedy accompanied him, as did Vice President Johnson and his wife, Lady Bird. The Kennedys planned to visit the Johnsons' ranch in the Texas Hill Country after a motorcade through Dallas.

On November 22, 1963, the president and the first lady waved and smiled from the backseat of a 1961 Lincoln Continental convertible that carried them through the Dallas streets. Texas governor John Connally and his wife, Nellie, close friends of the Johnsons, sat in front of the Kennedys in the limousine's jump seats. Secret Service agents followed in a separate car. Vice President Johnson and Lady Bird rode in the next car in line, two cars from the Kennedys. At 12:30 P.M. the motorcade turned onto Elm Street and passed in front of the Texas School Book Depository building. Shots rang out, and Kennedy, mortally wounded in the neck and the head, slumped down in his seat. Connally, also hit, shouted, "My God, they're going to kill us all!"

As the motorcade sped toward Parkland Hospital, the Secret Service agent in Johnson's car vaulted into the backseat and covered the vice president with his body to protect him. A team of doctors at Parkland, alerted by the Dallas Police Department, immediately began treating Kennedy and Connally as soon as the limousine arrived at the hospital doors. Connally underwent surgery and eventually recovered. Doctors working on Kennedy could find no pulse, and the president was declared dead at about 1:00 P.M.

Moments after this photograph was taken, President John F. Kennedy was assassinated, in Dallas, Texas, on November 22, 1963.

The Johnsons waited in the hospital for news of the president's condition. Shortly after receiving official word that Kennedy was dead, the Johnsons were taken back to Air Force One, the presidential plane, at Love Field in Dallas. Johnson ordered that the plane not take off for Washington until Jacqueline Kennedy and President Kennedy's body were on board.

Vice President Johnson takes the oath of office aboard Air Force One. To his right is Jacqueline Kennedy.

Johnson's old friend U.S. District Court judge Sarah T. Hughes administered the presidential oath of office aboard the plane at about 2:38 P.M., barely two hours after bullets struck Kennedy. After the oath a solemn Johnson kissed his wife, Lady Bird, then turned and kissed Kennedy's widow, Jacqueline, who also stood at his side. Then Johnson turned to the pilot and said, "Let's be airborne."

Back in Washington a somber Johnson told a waiting American public, "We have suffered a loss that cannot be weighed. For me it is a deep personal tragedy. . . . I will do my best. That is all I can do. I ask for your help—and God's."

That night he conferred with the inner circle who would advise him in the days ahead. Bill D. Moyers, a former aide and deputy director of the Peace Corps, and Walter Jenkins, Johnson's administrative assistant as vice president, moved into the White House the next day. Johnson met with members of Congress, the Kennedy family, the Cabinet, the Supreme Court, and the White House staff. He conferred with former presidents Dwight Eisenhower, Harry S. Truman, and Herbert Hoover. He asked that executive staff and members of the Cabinet remain in their posts. Senator J. William Fulbright described Johnson as "calm and contained" as he discussed foreign affairs with government officials.

THE PRESIDENCY

On November 27, 1963, just five days after he assumed the presidency, Johnson assured a jittery nation that he intended to continue Kennedy's work on civil rights and other initiatives. Johnson pledged to continue Kennedy's legacy by carrying on the fight for civil rights. In the televised address before a joint session of Congress, he declared that Congress could "honor President Kennedy's memory" by passing the civil rights bill "for which he fought so long."

He continued, "We have talked long enough in this country about equal rights. We have talked for one hundred years or more. It is time now to write the next chapter, and to write it in the books of law."

CIVIL RIGHTS (1964)

Despite Johnson's reassurances, many doubted whether a white southerner would push for civil rights legislation. Johnson had helped weaken Eisenhower's civil rights bill and had many connections to segregationists in Congress. But his closest allies knew that he meant business.

The House took up the **Civil Rights Act of 1964** in January. The bill greatly expanded protections of the rights of African Americans. It banned segregation in facilities open to the public, whether they were publicly or privately owned. The legislation also barred discrimination by unions, in jobs, and in programs receiving federal funds. Under the act's provisions the federal government was given the power to sue public schools that did not desegregate. The bill also extended the life of the Civil Rights Commission, allowed defendants who claimed their rights had been violated to get a hearing in federal court, and mandated that equal standards be required for black and white voters.

On a roll-call vote on February 10, 1964, the House passed the bill by a wide margin. Johnson praised the passage, which came on a vote of 290 for and 130 against, as a "historic step forward for the cause of human dignity in America."

The triumph, however, marked only the beginning of a tough battle to win passage for the bill. The Senate, controlled by old-time southern Democrats who opposed desegregation, posed the biggest hurdle. Unlike the House, the Senate allowed members to block legislation by conducting a **filibuster**. Senators using this technique could talk around the clock for days, weeks, and even months. They tied up the work of the Senate until one side or the other backed down. Stopping a filibuster required a two-thirds vote of the senators present and voting.

Johnson mounted an unrelenting campaign to pass the bill in the Senate. With the bill before them, segregationists carried out their threat and began a filibuster. Johnson called in favors, pulled strings, and worked with Senator Hubert Humphrey to rally support.

During the lengthy filibuster that followed, Johnson's team made sure supporters stayed on the Senate floor around the clock to prevent the opposite side from killing the bill. Finally, in May, Republican leader Everett Dirksen agreed to support the bill. On June 10, Dirksen brought in enough Republican votes to cut off the filibuster. The Senate then voted to pass the bill, 73 to 27.

President Johnson signs the Civil Rights Act of 1964, which protected the rights of African Americans, banned segregation, and prohibited discrimination in jobs and federal programs.

The final vote, held on June 19, 1964, came at the end of the longest debate in the Senate's history. The filibuster had gone on for fifty-seven days over a period of three months.

On July 2, 1964, the president signed the Civil Rights Act of 1964 into law. Johnson, a man of the South, had triumphed in his efforts to push through the most important and far-reaching civil rights bill in the history of the United States. Johnson, in announcing the passage, urged Americans to support the new law. He told them to "go to work in our communities and our States, in our homes and in our hearts, to eliminate the last vestiges of injustice in our beloved country." He pledged to enforce the law to protect civil rights.

In part, the feeling of loyalty to Kennedy among congressmen and their constituents helped win support for the measure, according to Congressman Hale Boggs. But he and others who witnessed the all-out effort Johnson and Humphrey devoted to the bill gave most of the credit to them.

"Johnson brought tremendous energy to his job," said Boggs. "It was amazing how hard he worked. I got the impression that the man never slept. He was, particularly at that time, very close to Congress, and he would see members constantly and would talk to them, persuade them."

CONTROVERSY AT THE DEMOCRATIC CONVENTION, 1964

In the summer of 1964 activists formed the Mississippi Freedom Democratic Party (MFDP) and launched a campaign—called Freedom Summer—to register African-American voters in Mississippi. Members of the Ku Klux Klan and other segregationists violently opposed the group's efforts. During that time sixty-five homes and churches in Mississippi were burned, at least eighty civil rights volunteers were severely beaten, and six people were murdered. The bodies of three volunteers—two white men from New York and a black man from Mississippi—were found on August 4, less than three weeks before the Democratic Convention was set to open in Atlantic City, New Jersey.

When MFDP members tried to participate in meetings, or caucuses, to elect delegates to the Democratic Convention, white segregationists who controlled the Democratic Party in

Aaron Henry, leader of the Mississippi Freedom Democratic Party, argues for seats at the national convention.

Mississippi blocked their way. Because they were shut out, the members of the MFDP set up their own caucuses and elected their own delegates to the convention. The convention opened August 24, 1964. When the MFDP delegates arrived, they demanded to be seated as regular delegates. The white Mississippi delegates made equal demands.

Heading into the 1964 election, Johnson walked a tightrope between southern leaders who favored segregation and black activist groups and their liberal supporters in the North who lobbied for civil rights. Johnson, Humphrey, and other party leaders feared that they would lose southern votes if they seated the MFDP delegates. They also were afraid that liberals and blacks would desert them if they did not allow MFDP delegates to participate. So they offered a compromise. The white delegates would be seated if they signed a pledge to support the ticket in the fall. In turn the MFDP delegation would get two at-large, nonvoting delegates and a promise that the party would not discriminate against blacks when certifying delegates at the next national convention in 1968. The compromise satisfied neither side. Both the MFDP and the white delegates from Mississippi walked out of the convention in protest.

PRESIDENTIAL ELECTION, 1964

Despite the controversy Johnson and Humphrey (the president's choice for vice president) came out of the convention confident they would win the election. The Republicans had named conservative Arizona senator Barry Goldwater to head their ticket in November. Some viewed Goldwater as a **right-wing extremist**. He pledged to do away with Social Security and other social welfare programs. Voters also feared he might use nuclear weapons against the Soviet Union.

As predicted, Johnson and Humphrey won a landslide victory over Goldwater—

Senator Barry Goldwater campaigns for president in Marietta, Ohio, in 1964. Many feared that Goldwater would approve the use of nuclear weapons against the U.S.S.R.

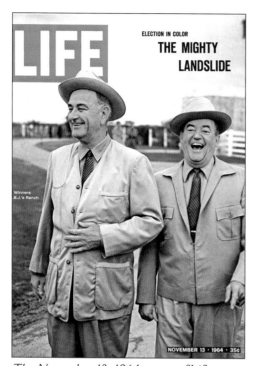

THE MIGHTY LANDSLIDE

ELECTION IN COLOR

LIFE

Winners .B.J.'s Ranch

NOVEMBER 13 · 1964 · 35¢

The November 13, 1964, cover of Life *featured President Johnson and Vice President Humphrey at Johnson's ranch in Texas. The headline refers to their victory in the election.*

61 percent to 38.5 percent. The landslide stands as the fourth-largest sweep in American presidential history. Forty-four states and the District of Columbia supported the Democratic ticket.

Some southerners opposed to civil rights stayed loyal to Johnson and campaigned for him. But the Democrats learned that fall they could no longer count on the South to deliver votes for their ticket. Alabama, South Carolina, Louisiana, Georgia, and Mississippi were the only states outside Goldwater's home state of Arizona that did not vote for Johnson and Humphrey that year.

Johnson's aide Bill Moyers told of the president's sad prediction after he had signed the Civil Rights Act of 1964. "I think we just delivered the South to the Republican Party for a long time to come," he had told Moyers. His words proved true. White southerners would not forgive Johnson or the Democratic Party for ending segregation. Beginning with the election of 1968, Republicans would claim southern votes for decades to come. In addition, disillusioned black activists—joined by antiwar protesters—would later demonstrate their frustrations with the Democrats during the violent clashes that disrupted the 1968 convention.

GREAT SOCIETY AND THE WAR ON POVERTY

Before the election, in January 1964, the president launched a "War on Poverty" to help poor Americans improve their standard of living. To head the new initiative, Johnson appointed Sargent Shriver, John F. Kennedy's brother-in-law and a practiced politician in his own right.

"You just make this thing work. Appoint all the committees you want to, confer with everybody," Johnson told Shriver. "This is number one on the domestic front. Next to peace in the world this is the most important."

After some initial resistance the 88th Congress agreed. Congress authorized $947.5 million in 1964 for the antipoverty program. Included were a job corps, a food-stamp program, a youth employment initiative, and other antipoverty measures.

Johnson came out of the 1964 elections with the huge advantage of having a two-thirds majority of Democrats in both the Senate and the House. Several Old South conservatives lost at the polls, and a number of liberals won seats in the 89th Congress. Johnson used this political advantage to win support for a broad collection of social programs designed to give Americans a hand getting out of poverty and moving toward a better life. The package—an expansion of the War on Poverty—included aid to education, protection of civil rights, urban renewal, Medicare, conservation, highway beautification, control and prevention of crime and delinquency, promotion of the arts, preservation of the environment, and consumer protection.

Johnson introduced his "Great Society" on the campaign trail in April 1964. During a four-state tour of areas blighted by poverty, the president pledged to "build a great society" in the

Sargent Shriver talks to a group of boys from Harlem in New York City about clearing rubble to make way for a new playground as part of an urban renewal program.

United States. He said his proposals would address such problems as discrimination, unemployment, the challenges of aging, the destruction of natural resources, and a "second-class system of education." Lady Bird Johnson, who also spoke at the rally, summed up Johnson's vision for a great American society. "In a country as free and rich as America, no one should be held back because he was born to a poor family, or in a poor neighborhood or because of the color of his skin," she said.

The president outlined his ambitious plan during the state of the union address delivered to Congress and the nation on January 4, 1965. Before the end of the month Johnson presented

Congress with a $99.7 billion budget that called for increases in spending for education, health, benefits for the poor and the unemployed, antipoverty programs, Social Security, job training, and economic development in run-down areas. The *New York Times* called Johnson's proposed measures "the biggest expansion of domestic welfare and educational programs since the New Deal of the 1930s." Republican leaders in Congress had little to say about the increases in funding and programs. Republican senator Everett Dirksen suggested cuts in foreign aid and the military but remained silent on the funds devoted to social programs.

Congress prepared to consider the mountain of legislation involved in carrying out Johnson's vision of a Great Society. Humphrey spoke optimistically about the outcome. "This Congress is building a solid, lasting base for American progress and growth," he told a meeting of newspaper editors. Humphrey predicted Congress "will do more for the lasting long-term health of this nation than any Congress since the 73rd [under Franklin D. Roosevelt]."

One of the administration's first victories came on March 3, 1965, with the passage of a $1.1 billion bill to aid eleven states in the Appalachian Mountains. The funds were slated to pay for new roads, health centers, schools, restoration of land destroyed by mining, and timber industry development. A large Democratic majority, joined by moderate Republicans, killed efforts to modify or delay the passage of the bill.

Other initiatives soon followed. By the end of March Johnson had "unloaded a whole truckload of proposals on Capitol Hill," according to a White House insider. Among them were a $1.3 billion education bill, which the House approved on March 26 by

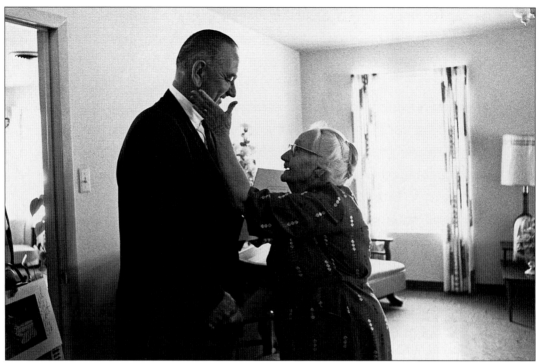

An elderly woman shows her appreciation to President Johnson for his signing of the Medicare health care bill, which provided medical coverage for older Americans.

a 263 to 153 margin; a Medicare bill to provide health care for the nation's elderly; and a bill that provided rent subsidies for moderate- and low-income families.

Under Johnson's leadership, Congress passed more progressive legislation between 1964 and 1968 than Franklin Roosevelt had in his New Deal. "It was a Congress of accomplished hopes," said speaker of the House John W. McCormack, "a Congress of realized dreams."

Representative Hale Boggs said Congress during that time "passed an enormous amount of legislation. In the field of health, for instance, we passed more bills than had ever been passed in all the rest of history of the country put together. Same thing in the field of education, conservation, water pollution, air pollution, and so on."

Voting Rights Act of 1965

In 1965 southern violence against African-American activists continued as segregationists resisted the reforms mandated by the Civil Rights Act. Despite a voting-rights section in the Civil Rights Act, state and local officials in the South continued to use literacy requirements and other methods to keep African Americans from voting. In March Johnson proposed the Voting Rights Act of 1965. The act would ban such requirements and ensure that all citizens had the right to vote. He pushed through the vote on the bill after television news programs showed film of officials in Selma, Alabama, beating voting-rights demonstrators led by Martin Luther King Jr.

Southern leaders in the Senate again led a filibuster, but the recent election had depleted their ranks. Republican Senator Dirksen and Vice President Humphrey led a bipartisan coalition that helped draft and then pass the legislation.

African-American women in Alabama vote for the first time after the enactment of the Voting Rights Act.

Great Society Programs

President Lyndon Johnson's Great Society opened doors and provided benefits for millions of Americans. It also worked to protect consumers, the environment, travelers, and borrowers. Among the many programs, agencies, and laws established during Johnson's term of office were the following:

- Medicare, health benefits for the elderly
- Elementary and Secondary Education Act, federal funds for schools
- Department of Housing and Urban Development
- Highway Beautification Act, promoted by Lady Bird Johnson
- Urban renewal programs
- School breakfast programs
- Food stamps
- Head Start
- Housing subsidies
- Block grants for state and city law enforcement agencies
- Voting rights and elimination of poll tax and literacy requirements
- Water Quality Act of 1965 and Clean Water Restoration Act of 1966
- Clean Air Act and Air Quality Acts of 1965 and 1967
- Solid Waste Disposal Act of 1965
- Expansion of national parks and creation of small urban parks

- Meat Inspection Act of 1967
- Wholesale Poultry Products Act of 1968
- National Commission on Product Safety
- Truth in Lending Act of 1968
- Traffic Highway Safety Act (requiring seat belts in cars, among other safety measures)
- Teacher Corps Act of 1965, easing the teacher shortage in poor areas
- Adult Education Act of 1968, funds for classes for adults
- Job Corps and Neighborhood Youth Corps
- Educational Opportunity Act of 1968, college aid for the poor
- Medicaid, health benefits for the poor
- Federally funded training for doctors and nurses
- Establishment of mental health centers
- Immunizations for preschool children
- Health centers focusing on heart ailments, cancer, and stroke

On August 6 a beaming Johnson signed the bill in the room where Lincoln had signed a bill freeing slaves serving in the Confederate Army. Johnson promised that the federal government would take swift action in states discriminating against voters. He also announced that the attorney general would file suits against four states that charged a fee (a poll tax) to discourage black voters. "Today is a triumph for freedom as huge as any victory won on any battlefield," he said. "Today we strike away the last major shackle of those fierce and ancient bonds."

Better Lives for Americans

Many of Johnson's programs made great strides in improving the lives of ordinary Americans. In some cases they changed the political direction of America. When the Voting Rights Act was passed in 1965, there were only three hundred African-American officials in the entire nation, according to Dr. Joseph E. Lowery. Lowery was among the founding members, along with Martin Luther King Jr., of the Southern Christian Leadership Conference, a civil rights group that worked to increase voter registration among blacks. In 2005, Lowery said, African Americans filled almost ten thousand official posts.

Beginning in the 1960s and for several years after Johnson's initiatives were adopted, the poverty rate in the United States dipped dramatically. It went from 22.4 percent in the late 1950s to 11.1 percent in 1973, decreasing by more than half. Programs of the Kennedy and Johnson administrations created 10.5 million jobs in seven and a half years, salaries and wages increased, business profits rose, and unemployment fell below 3.8 percent. Wilbur J. Cohen, Secretary of Health, Education, and Welfare under Johnson, told the *New York Times* in 1968 that "the United States can eliminate poverty in the coming decade and go on to assure adequate income for the overwhelming majority of Americans."

Black Power and Riots in the Streets

Unfortunately, that overly optimistic prediction did not come true. "He [Johnson] had promised the impoverished much more than he could deliver," said an expert on the presidency. "How are you ever going to create a society which has no poverty at all?"

As a result, people—African Americans in particular—began to lose faith in Johnson. They wanted immediate change.

Tensions grew as African Americans in America's urban ghettos began to demand better treatment. The civil rights activists of the 1950s and early 1960s, under Martin Luther King Jr.'s leadership, used nonviolent ways—sit-ins and marches—to make their demands heard. But some of the angry young inner-city leaders did not rule out using violence to accomplish their goals.

Stokely Carmichael, a leader in the Student Nonviolent Coordinating Committee, among others, began to agitate for "**black power**." Black power was a movement that demanded equal rights for black Americans and called for blacks themselves to take control of their own lives. Carmichael told his followers, "I am not going to beg the white man for anything I deserve. I'm going to take it."

Johnson had hoped that the civil rights bill and the vast network of social programs would break the color barrier and lift Americans out of poverty. And in fact, during the 1960s segregation in public places ended, and the number of poor Americans steadily decreased.

However, other factors began to wear away at the Great Society. A more conservative Congress eliminated some of the programs and cut funds for others. Continuing violence and riots in the nation's cities made it harder for Johnson to convince voters and

Stokely Carmichael speaks to a crowd during the March Against Fear rally at the Mississippi State Capital in June 1966.

Rioting in the Streets

On August 11, 1965, Los Angeles police arrested a young black man for drunken driving. His mother confronted the police, and a struggle took place between officers and black onlookers. Rumors about the incident flashed through Watts, a troubled section of the city occupied mainly by blacks. Many in the neighborhood lived in poverty. They were unemployed or worked at low-paying jobs. Schools in the neighborhood had little funding, houses were run-down, and racial tensions and police brutality flared.

The incident unleashed a storm of pent-up anger. Black youths smashed store windows and tossed flaming, gasoline-filled bottles, setting buildings on fire. Looters ran through ransacked businesses, grabbing furniture, clothing, food, guns, and anything else they could find. Rioters dragged people from cars and beat them. Snipers shot at police, and officers and National Guardsmen tried to enforce a curfew in an area of three thousand city blocks.

The riots that erupted lasted five days, left thirty-six dead and hundreds injured, destroyed 232 businesses and damaged 632 others, and caused an estimated $175 million in damages. Police arrested almost four thousand people, including many African Americans in their early teens.

Some black militants referred to the riots as a revolt by blacks against whites. They used it to gain recruits in the black power movement. Other leaders, black and white, condemned the violence. But they also

denounced conditions in Watts. Johnson spoke of "the bitter years that preceded the riots, the death of hope where hope existed, their sense of failure to change the conditions of life."

Riots followed in equally troubled areas of America's cities that summer and for the next three years. Between 1965 and 1968 more than three hundred riots raged in Washington, D.C.; Newark, New Jersey; Detroit, Michigan; Baltimore, Maryland; Cleveland, Ohio; and many other cities.

Congress to help poor blacks. People did not want to "reward" black rioters with federal programs. The riots also gave white southerners another reason not to support Johnson. Their anger over desegregation had already caused many to leave the Democratic Party. That weakened Johnson's base of power and the party's hold on the South.

Protests against the Vietnam War also began to undercut Johnson's ability to lead. Even King—who had worked closely with Johnson during the Watts riot and the passage of the Civil Rights Act—complained that the Vietnam War took money and attention away from needed domestic programs. The president, King charged in December 1966, had let Vietnam become a "national obsession," while the War on Poverty had become nothing more than a "skirmish."

Vietnam War

America's entanglement in Vietnam began long before Johnson took office. The conflict had its beginnings in the cold war between the United States and the Soviet Union. As in Korea, the U.S.S.R. supported communist forces in northern Vietnam, while America supported the government based in the south.

President Harry S. Truman sent military advisers to the region in 1950. In 1956 President Dwight D. Eisenhower dispatched a team of American advisers to train South Vietnamese soldiers. Eisenhower believed in the Domino Theory—that if the United States allowed communists to control North Vietnam, other countries in the region would soon be overrun. Those countries, too, he believed, would fall to communism, just like dominoes.

In the early 1960s President John F. Kennedy sent more than 16,000 military advisers to Vietnam and approved $400 million in military aid. In early November 1963 Kennedy supported South Vietnamese generals who took over the government of that country in a military coup.

Just before the 1964 Democratic Convention, on August 2 and August 4, Johnson received word that North Vietnamese torpedo boats had fired on a U.S. destroyer. The U.S. vessel was in international waters in the Gulf of Tonkin, off the coast of North Vietnam. After the report of the attack, Secretary of Defense Robert McNamara and Johnson's national security advisers recommended that he order air strikes in retaliation. He did so, then spoke to the nation during a near-midnight broadcast, informing the public of the incident and the response. As Johnson began his late-night speech to the nation, the planes he had unleashed had just about reached their North Vietnamese target.

The next day Johnson asked Congress to grant him the authority to take "all necessary measures" against the North Vietnamese to fend off future attacks. Based on the Johnson administration's report of the Tonkin Bay incident, Congress issued a joint resolution on August 7 giving the president the power he requested—and that later would allow him to escalate the war. However, in a tape of McNamara's August 3, 1964, telephone call to the president, the defense secretary can be heard acknowledging that a covert U.S. operation in the area could have provoked the attack by the North Vietnamese. "There's no question but that had bearing on it," McNamara told the president. Later investigation raised questions about whether the attack ever happened at all.

Nonetheless, the attack—real or fabricated—sparked the rapid escalation of the war. Johnson ordered Operation Rolling Thunder in February 1965. The mission directed bombing raids on North Vietnam that would continue for the next three years. The first American combat troops arrived in Vietnam in March. General William Westmoreland, commander of U.S. forces in Vietnam, advised Johnson that if he did not send more troops, he would lose the war. In response, the president sent 50,000 soldiers to Vietnam in July. At the war's peak the United States had about half a million troops in Vietnam.

U.S. soldiers disembark in South Vietnam.

Vietnam Quagmire

By the spring of 1965 President Johnson's advisers were all reporting that South Vietnam was about to collapse. A frustrated Johnson said he felt "like a hitchhiker caught in a hailstorm on a Texas highway. I can't run, I can't hide, and I can't make it stop."

As the months passed, the situation grew worse. Johnson agonized about what to do. The president had tried to keep the enemy at bay without risking the lives of more American soldiers. He had ordered the bombing of bridges and the enemy's ammunition dumps and radar stations. "I've tried to keep it to that," he said, "so I won't escalate it and get into trouble with China and with Russia. . . . I don't want to be a warmonger."

But military leaders told him that was not enough. In July 1965 General William Westmoreland, the commander of U.S. troops in Vietnam, urged the president to send more soldiers to the front. Johnson knew an escalation would mean that more American soldiers would die. Such an action would anger many Americans. Congress would not be pleased either if he ordered more troops without consulting them. He knew, however, that if he brought the issue to Congress, there would be a long debate on the country's involvement in the conflict.

Others were urging that the United States withdraw completely and leave Vietnam on its own. Johnson did not feel he could do that. He told Martin Luther King Jr.:

(continued)

If I pulled out, I think that our commitments would be no good anywhere. I didn't get us into this . . . [but] I don't want to pull down the flag and come home running with my tail between my legs, particularly if it's going to create more problems. . . . So I've got a pretty tough problem, and I'm not all wise. I pray every night to get direction and judgment and leadership that permit me to do what's right.

Finally, on July 28, 1965, Johnson ordered 50,000 more troops into Vietnam. "We do not want an expanding struggle with consequences that no one can foresee," he told the American people. "But we will not surrender. And we will not retreat."

The effort failed to bring victory.

Although the majority of the American people still supported the war in 1966, opposition to it was growing. The war had brought increased inflation, resistance to the draft, stalled wages and labor strikes, rising taxes, and worldwide criticism of U.S. foreign policy. A frustrated Johnson told Martin Luther King Jr., who had begun to question the president's stance on the war, "I want peace as much as you do, and more so, because I am the fellow that wakes up in the morning with a report that fifty of our boys died last night. These [North Vietnamese] folks just will not come to the conference table."

Anti-Vietnam War protesters march down Pennsylvania Avenue during a rally in Washington, D.C., in 1969.

JOHNSON AND THE PRESS

Lyndon Johnson had a complicated relationship with the press. From his earliest days as a campaigner, he recognized the power of the press and used publicity to his advantage whenever he could.

His folksy ways, colorful language, and sometimes bizarre actions made him a favorite subject among the media. At times Johnson's urge

to "let it all hang out" backfired. Papers around the world prominently featured a photograph of Johnson lifting his shirt to reveal the scar from his 1965 gall bladder surgery. Apparently Johnson had thought his action would reassure Americans that their president had weathered surgery just fine. This too-intimate picture of the president's health brought more ridicule than relief.

During the Vietnam War Johnson's resentment against what he saw as a biased press grew deeper. Reporters began writing about the "credibility gap" caused by an administration that left out—or distorted—key information that might be seen as politically damaging. Johnson's critics complained that his answers were unrealistically optimistic. A frustrated Johnson, though, blamed the press for being too negative. He commented, "If one morning, I walked on top of the water, across the Potomac River, the headline that afternoon would read, PRESIDENT CAN'T SWIM."

RISING DOUBTS

As the war worsened, the president evaded questions from the press. The press, covering the war firsthand, began to point out discrepancies between what they saw and what Johnson told the American public. The widening credibility gap undermined Johnson's effectiveness as a leader. People no longer believed what the president said.

Martin Luther King Jr. publicly declared his opposition to the war, and in a March 31, 1968, press conference King told reporters he would support Robert Kennedy or Eugene McCarthy instead of the president in the upcoming elections. Both men had declared their candidacy for the party's nomination.

Johnson became increasingly bitter over what he saw as a betrayal by his former friends and allies. He could not understand why the people he had done so much to help—African Americans and the poor—had turned on him.

According to historian Doris Kearns Goodwin, Johnson asked:

> *How is it possible that all these people could be so ungrateful to me after I had given them so much? . . . I spilled my guts out in getting the Civil Rights Act of 1964 through Congress. . . . I tried to make it possible for every child of every color to grow up in a nice house, to eat a solid breakfast, to attend a decent school, and to get a good and lasting job. . . . I fought on [students'] behalf for scholarships and loans and grants. I fought for better teachers and better schools.*

But instead of giving thanks, Johnson complained, blacks rioted in the streets, students chanted anti-Johnson slogans, and the poor idolized John F. Kennedy.

On March 31, 1968, a defeated Johnson told Lady Bird and two guests, "I do not believe I can unite this country." Later that evening the president delivered an address on the war's progress and announced a major shift in policy. As a step toward peace, he revealed that he had ordered an end to U.S. bombings in almost

The strain of the presidency is evident as President Johnson prepares an address on troop deployment and new actions in Southeast Asia.

all areas of Vietnam and called on North Vietnamese leader Ho Chi Minh to participate in peace talks. His next statement truly stunned the nation: "I shall not seek, and I will not accept, the nomination of my party for another term as your President."

LYNDON B. JOHNSON'S LEGACY

*T*he remaining days of Johnson's presidency were haunted by Vietnam and violence. Peace talks between the United States and North Vietnam began in May 1968, but they soon came to a standstill. In April an assassin's bullet killed civil rights leader Martin Luther King Jr. during a rally in Memphis, Tennessee. Two months later the former attorney general Robert F. Kennedy was gunned down while he was on the campaign trail. His assassination, like that of his brother and King, shocked a nation already sickened by violence.

In August 1968 violent clashes between Chicago police and antiwar protesters disrupted the Democratic Convention. In response to the protests and to those of black activists, the Democrats revised their convention rules and opened the process to many new participants. The divisive convention, however, damaged the Democrats' chances during the presidential election. Republican Richard M. Nixon and segregationist governor George Wallace of Alabama split the southern vote. Only Johnson's home state of Texas and West Virginia among the southern states voted for Vice President Hubert H. Humphrey, the Democratic candidate. Humphrey also won support from several northern states, but he ultimately lost, with 42.7 percent of the popular vote to Nixon's 43.4 percent.

In January 1969 South Vietnam and the Viet Cong (the guerrilla force in the south supported by North Vietnam) joined in peace talks just after Johnson left office. The war ended for most Americans when the United States, North Vietnam, the Viet Cong, and South Vietnam signed a cease-fire agreement in January 1973. By March of that year all U.S. ground troops had been evacuated from the region. Helicopters lifted the last American military personnel out of South Vietnam on April 29, 1975, as Saigon, its capital, fell to the North Vietnamese in the final stages of the war.

By the war's end more than 58,000 American soldiers had been killed and another 300,000 had been wounded. An estimated 4 million civilians in Vietnam and more than 1 million Vietnamese soldiers died in the war.

U.S. Marines move out of South Vietnam in July 1969. By the early 1970s all U.S. ground troops were out of the region.

The End of an Era

During the Depression, President Franklin D. Roosevelt's New Deal helped pull America out of despair. For the next forty years the American people looked to the government to help solve the nation's ills. The majority of Americans held the liberal viewpoint that government programs could improve the economy, help the disadvantaged, and find remedies for racial injustice.

Lyndon Johnson embraced this belief and became its champion, with the help of a willing Congress. Democrats, many of whom were liberals, made up the majority. Moderate Republicans helped offset conservative southern Democrats. Under Johnson's leadership, Congress enacted the largest collection of government programs ever proposed to aid Americans. His Great Society covered a huge range of issues, from civil rights for blacks to environmental conservation to education. With Johnson's successes, liberals reached their highest point.

At the same time, however, Johnson's failures marked the end of liberals' power. The battle over civil rights and segregation split the Democrats and weakened Johnson's strength as leader of the party. Racial unrest and urban riots eroded support for his social programs. Johnson's failures in Vietnam drove away liberals and other backers. When Johnson stepped down from the presidency, his downfall meant the end of liberalism and the American belief in government as problem-solver.

A Visionary Leader

Lyndon Johnson retired to his beloved Texas ranch in January 1969. Politics had been his life for forty years. He had dominated powerful men and had fought for righteous causes. In retirement, Johnson lost his center. He gained weight and began smoking again, a habit he had given up after his 1955 heart attack.

On January 22, 1973, he suffered a massive heart attack at his Texas ranch and died at age sixty-four. Shortly before 4:00 P.M., Johnson called Secret Service agents at the ranch for help. When they arrived, they tried to revive him

President Johnson retired to his ranch after leaving the presidency.

but with no results. He was taken by plane to San Antonio, where he was pronounced dead. A remarkable life ended that day.

Even in death Johnson sparked controversy among his fellow Americans. Many marked his passing with bitterness over the toll taken by a war finally winding down. Decades later the taint of the Vietnam War still cling to the legacy of Lyndon B. Johnson. Liberals and moderates often overlook his contribution to the causes they have embraced—civil rights, education, the war against poverty—and see only the stain of the Vietnam War.

Johnson's performance in Vietnam undoubtedly marred his overall record as a great president. But it cannot erase his gains in civil rights and the great strides Johnson made with his Great Society programs to ease poverty and injustice. The Great Society programs Johnson pushed through Congress, said one expert in presidential affairs, "rival the New Deal and make Johnson [in the minds of historians] one of the great visionary presidents in domestic affairs of American history, maybe the greatest."

Many of the Great Society programs have become a permanent part of federal governmental policy: Head Start, Community Action Programs, VISTA, Medicare, Medicaid, public radio and public television, housing subsidies, education loans and grants, federal funds for schools, clean air and water laws, and environmental protection measures.

Johnson's severest critics charge that he dramatically enlarged the federal bureaucracy and increased tax burdens on Americans. When President Dwight D. Eisenhower left office, the federal government operated about forty-five social welfare programs to serve Americans' needs. At the end of Johnson's presidency 435 federal social welfare programs were in place.

His supporters counter that the agencies and programs Johnson put in place have greatly improved the lives of millions of Americans. Until Franklin D. Roosevelt's New Deal the American people had seen the government only as an agency that enforced rules, according to Joseph Califano, who served as Johnson's senior domestic policy aide. FDR set up Social Security and other benefits for citizens. Johnson's administration struck down social injustice and offered people improvements in education, health care, and jobs. Lyndon Johnson, Califano said, transformed the government into a tool to help people.

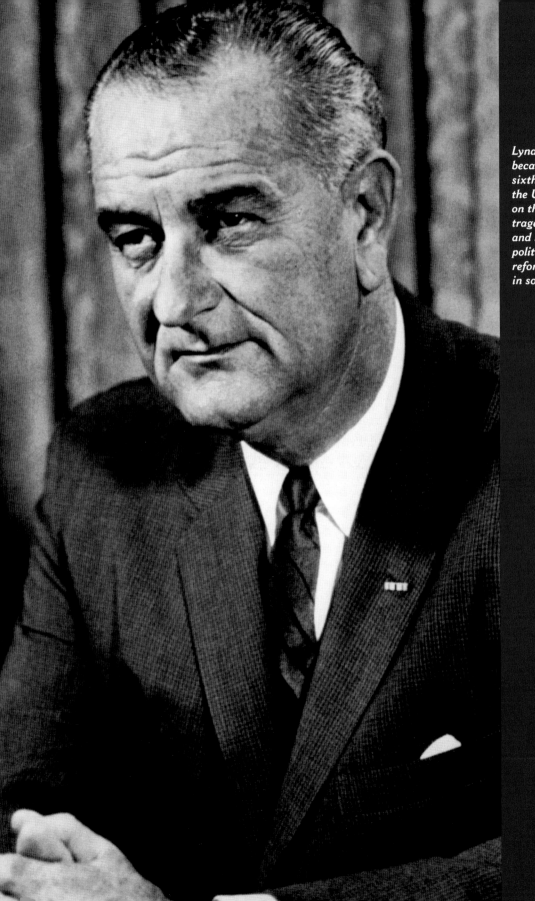

Lyndon B. Johnson became the thirty-sixth president of the United States on the coattails of tragedy. His skill and strength in politics led to great reforms and gains in social justice.

TIMELINE

1908
Born August 27 in Stonewall, Texas

1930
Graduates from Southwest Texas State Teachers College

1931
Begins job as private secretary to U.S. Congressman Richard Kleberg

1934
Marries Claudia "Lady Bird" Taylor

1937
Elected to House of Representatives in a special election

1941
Enlists in the navy

1948
Elected to Senate

1953
Elected minority leader of the Senate

1900

1955
Elected majority leader of the Senate

1960
Loses bid to run as Democratic candidate for president; accepts John F. Kennedy's offer to run as vice president and wins

1963
Becomes president after the assassination of President John F. Kennedy

1964
Reelected president; pushes through Civil Rights Act of 1964

1965
Introduces Great Society package to Congress

1968
Announces he will not run for reelection

1973
Dies January 22 in Texas

1980

GLOSSARY

black power political movement in the 1960s formed by African Americans who pushed for civil rights through nonviolent and sometimes violent actions

caucus meeting of members of the Democratic or Republican parties at which delegates to the National Convention are elected. Also refers to leadership committees in Congress that direct party activities in the House and Senate.

Civil Rights Act of 1964 landmark legislation that outlawed segregation in American public schools and all public places. It also banned discrimination in unions, in government programs, and in jobs.

constituents voters in a congressman's or a senator's district

credit obtaining goods on the promise to pay for them later

Democratic and Republican National Conventions gathering of the Democratic or Republican parties at which members (or delegates) choose their candidates for president and vice president

Democratic and Republican Policy Committees groups that help develop policy for each political party. The committees fill a variety of roles, from researching and reporting on issues for party members to tracking roll-call votes and scheduling hearings on bills before Congress.

federal subsidies money provided by the federal government to help pay for projects and programs, such as housing for the poor and the building of dams and other large construction projects

filibuster a method used by senators to block or delay action on a bill or other matter by debating it nonstop. A vote of two thirds of the members present is required to stop the debate.

Great Society the name President Lyndon B. Johnson gave to a collection of social welfare programs designed to eliminate poverty, guarantee civil rights, and improve the environment and the lives of Americans

majority leader and minority leader (also called floor leaders) in the Senate the leader of a political party who serves as the party's chief spokesman and coordinates the party's position on the issues that go before the Senate. The majority leader is from the party with the most members in the Senate; the minority leader's party has fewer members in the senate.

New Deal President Franklin D. Roosevelt's collection of programs to aid Americans during the Great Depression of the 1930s. Social Security was created as part of the New Deal.

primaries elections in which Democratic or Republican voters choose the candidate who will represent their party in the general election. In rare cases other parties (besides the Democratic or Republican) hold primaries.

right-wing extremist a person or group with views much more conservative than those held by the majority of people

stock market an institution through which shares of businesses (stocks) are bought and sold

War on Poverty series of programs proposed by President Lyndon B. Johnson to help poor people and eliminate poverty

whip in the Senate an assistant to the majority or minority leader who helps round up votes within the party on major issues

FURTHER INFORMATION

BOOKS

Levy, Debbie. *The Vietnam War* (Chronicle of America's Wars). Minneapolis, MN: Lerner Publishing Group, 2004.

Mayer, Robert H. *The Civil Rights Act of 1964* (At Issue in History). San Diego, CA: Greenhaven Press, 2004.

Morris-Lipsman, Arlene. *Presidential Races: The Battle for Power in the United States* (People's History). Minneapolis, MN: Twenty-First Century Books, 2007.

Pach, Chester J. *The Johnson Years* (Presidential Profiles). New York: Facts on File, 2005.

Rice, Earle. *Point of No Return: Tonkin Gulf and the Vietnam War* (First Battles). Greensboro, NC: Morgan Reynolds Publishing, 2003.

Sherman, Josepha. *The Cold War* (Chronicles of America's Wars). Minneapolis, MN: Lerner Publishing Group, 2003.

Williams, Jean Kinney. *Lyndon B. Johnson: America's 36th President* (Encyclopedia of Presidents, Second Series). Danbury, CT: Children's Press, 2005.

Wright, Susan. *The Civil Rights Act of 1964: Landmark Antidiscrimination Legislation*. New York: Rosen Central, 2005.

Web Sites

The American President: Lyndon Baines Johnson

http://www.millercenter.virginia.edu/index.php/academic/
americanpresident/lbjohnson

This site offers access to speeches, essays, private and public papers, multimedia presentations, and Lyndon Johnson's White House tapes.

The Lyndon Baines Johnson Library and Museum

http://www.lbjlib.utexas.edu

Oral histories by many of Lyndon Johnson's friends and associates, speeches, tapes, and multimedia presentations are available on this site. There is also a section on Lady Bird Johnson, which includes selections from her White House diary.

The Presidential Timeline of the Twentieth Century

http://www.presidentialtimeline.org

This Web site serves as a central access point to all twelve presidential libraries at the National Archives in Washington, D.C.

U.S. Senate

http://www.senate.gov/artandhistory/history/common/generic/
People_Leaders_Johnson.htm

The U.S. Senate's Art and History Web page provides a detailed biography of Lyndon Baines Johnson.

BIBLIOGRAPHY

Adler, Margot. "Activists Recall Drive for Voting Rights." *All Things Considered*, National Public Radio, August 6, 2005.

Barber, Stephan N. "Image of an Assassin: A New Look at the Zapruder Film." http://mcadams.posc.mu.edu/looking.htm. Accessed September 2, 2007.

Califano, Joseph A. Jr. *The Triumph & Tragedy of Lyndon Johnson*. New York: Simon & Schuster, 1991.

———. "What Was Really Great About the Great Society," *Washington Monthly*, October 1999. http://www.washingtonmonthly .com/features/1999/9910.califano.html. Accessed September 2, 2007.

Caro, Robert. *The Years of Lyndon Johnson: The Path to Power*. New York: Vintage Books, 1990.

———. *Master of the Senate*. New York: Alfred A. Knopf, 2002.

———. *The Years of Lyndon Johnson, Means of Ascent*. New York: Vintage Books, 1991.

Cooper, Stephen. Lyndon Johnson's Press Conferences, 1980. Education Resources Information Center. http://www.eric.ed.gov. Accessed September 2, 2007.

Dallek, Robert. *Lone Star Rising: Lyndon Johnson and His Times 1908–1960*. New York: Oxford University Press, 1991.

———. *Flawed Giant: Lyndon Johnson and His Times 1961–1975*. New York: Oxford University Press, 1998.

Department of the Navy. "Commander Lyndon B. Johnson, USNR."
Naval Historical Center, Washington, D.C. http://www.history.navy.mil/
faqs/faq60-6.htm. Accessed September 2, 2007.

Evans, Rowland, and Robert Novak. *Lyndon B. Johnson: The Exercise of
Power*. New York: New American Library, 1966.

Goodwin, Doris Kearns. *Lyndon Johnson and the American Dream*. New
York: St. Martin's Press, 1991.

"The Gulf of Tonkin." The Presidential Timeline of the Twentieth
Century. http://www.presidentialtimeline.org/html/exhibits.php?id=6
Accessed September 3, 2007.

Johnson, Lyndon Baines. *The Vantage Point, Perspectives of the Presidency
1963–1969*. New York: Holt, Rinehart and Winston, 1971.

Johnson, Lyndon Baines and Lady Bird Johnson. Tapes, diaries, reports,
and speeches. Lyndon Baines Johnson Library. http://www.lbjlib
.utexas.edu/johnson/ archives.hom. Accessed September 2, 2007.

Kotz, Nick. *Judgment Days*. New York: Houghton Mifflin Company, 2005.

"Lady Bird Johnson." *At the Epicenter*. Public Broadcasting System
special, November 1963–January 1965. http://www.pbs.org/
ladybird/epicenter/epicenter_report_assassination.html.
Accessed September 4, 2007.

New York Times articles, 1937–2007. Oral History Interviews, Internet
Copy, LBJ Library. http://www.lbjlib.utexas.edu/johnson/
archives.hom/biopage.asp/ Accessed September 4, 2007.

"Report of the President's Commission on the Assassination of President Kennedy." Washington, D.C.: U.S. Government Printing Office, 1964.

Schlutz, Stanley K. "The Almost Great Society: The 1960s," *American History 102*, Lecture 27. University of Wisconsin.

Shesol, Jeff. *Mutual Contempt: Lyndon Johnson, Robert Kennedy, and the Feud That Defined a Decade*. New York: W. W. Norton & Company, 1997.

Unger, Irwin and Debi. *LBJ, A Life*. Hoboken, NJ: John Wiley & Sons Inc., 1999.

U.S. Senate. "Senate Leaders: Lyndon B. Johnson, Master of the Senate." http://www.senate.gov/artandhistory/history/common/generic/People_ Leaders_Johnson.htm. Accessed September 4, 2007.

White House. "First Ladies: Claudia Taylor (Lady Bird) Johnson. http://www.whitehouse.gov/history/firstladies/cj36.html. Accessed September 4, 2007.

Zeitz, Joshua. "Democratic Debacle," *American Heritage*, July 2004, 62.

INDEX

Pages in **boldface** are illustrations.

ABOUT THE AUTHOR

Susan Dudley Gold has written almost four dozen books for middle school and high school students on a variety of topics, including American history, health issues, law, and space.

She has written several titles in the Supreme Court Milestones series for Marshall Cavendish Benchmark.

She and her husband, John Gold, own and operate a Web design and publishing business in Maine. They have one son, Samuel.